LIZ HOUGHTON

STILL MORE RHYMES

LIZ HOUGHTON

STILL MORE RHYMES

Life's peculiarities continue to provoke comment

© Liz Houghton 2023

Table of Subjects

Part 1: Miscellaneous

Here you will find a rag tag of assorted verses which reflect my haphazard approach to life as I go off on one of my many tangents, often prompted by current affairs.

Part 2: The International Collection

What's All This Then?

I need to give you some background information before you read this batch of poems.

In 2019, I was browsing the internet and came across YouTube footage of the first ever PingPongParkinson World Championships for people with Parkinson's. I was intrigued and wistful – I would love to have a go at that, but it was taking place in New York, somewhat out of my range. PingPongParkinson (PPP) was a new organisation founded by American/Croatian musician, Nenad Bach who had been diagnosed with Parkinson's. At first, this seemed to be the end of his live guitar performances, until he made the discovery that playing table tennis appeared to free him up enough to resume playing his guitar. To cut a long story short, Nenad is now on a global mission to spread the word and travels thousands of miles encouraging people with Parkinson's to get involved, not just with the sport, but also with each other to build a worldwide Parkinson's family. In 2019 the first PPP World Championships in Westchester, New York saw 61 athletes representing 12 countries take part. By 2022 and the third World Championships held in Pula, Croatia, the number had grown to 165 participants representing 20 countries. PPP clubs are springing up all over the world. In Europe, it has really taken off. In Germany there are currently 157 clubs catering for some 900 players.

Meanwhile, early in 2021, Gerry and I came across an article on the Table Tennis England website which talked about someone in Ipswich who was keen to spread the table tennis word amongst the Parkinson's community. He was trying to get a team together to represent England at the 2021 German Open, followed a week later by the World Championships in Berlin. We got in touch, and the rest, as they say, is history. I was going to Germany!

Part 3: Parkinson's

This is where I've pulled together all the poems I've written so far about Parkinson's Disease, so if you've read Volumes 1 and 2, forgive me for repeating them here. Putting them all together charts my progression through the condition which might be of interest.

Note:

At the bottom of some of the poems I have added an explanatory note.

Part 1

Miscellaneous

	Page
It's Christmas, Don't Panic ….…………...	1
Christmas is Coming ………..…………	2
Happy Christmas Everyone..……………...	3
Special Delivery…………………….…..	4
At Your Service………………………...	5
Doh! …………………………………..…...	7
Bojo ……………………………………...	8
Go Bojo, Go!……………………………...	9
Partygate ………………………….…..	10
Guilty as Charged..……………………..	11
Hasta la vista, Baby!…..………………..	12
Piracy Diplomacy……...………………..	13
Matt Finish ……………………………..	14
Mr and Mrs Dishy Rishi.…………….…..	16
PM………………………………….…...	17
Good Luck Liz……………………….…..	18
Not So Great Britain………………….…..	19
Bon Voyage……………………………...	20
Sports Day …..……………………….....	21
It's Not Funny (or clever)…………………	23
Remotely Controlled……………………...	25
Gadget Man ……………………………...	27
A Waiter's Tale …………………….…...	28
Bonkers ………………………………....	29
Hang on a Minute………………………...	30
Dressing Down ………………………….	31
Who Cares ……………………………...	33
Be Careful…………………………….…..	34
You What…………………………….…..	35
Boy to Man……………………………...	37
All Washed Up…………………………..	38
The Other Woman………………………...	39

xi

Cake	40
Crumbs	41
What's Brewing	42
Halloween	43
When The Balloon Goes Up	44
Gloom	45
Adverse Adverts	46
The Handcart	47
Perfect Storm	48
Modern Living	50
Tighten Your Belts	51
Cooee	52
Sixty Not Out	53
Number Three	54
Supermarket Checkout	55
God Save the Queen	56
QE2 RIP	57

It's Christmas, Don't Panic!

Deck the halls with boughs of holly.
No, this Yuletide won't be jolly.
Containers stuck in Felixstowe,
Sausage stocks are very low,
Turkeys hope they're off the hook,
You wonder what you're going to cook.
Supermarket shelves have gaps,
We'll be reduced to eating scraps,
Millions of girls and boys
May have to go without new toys.
The problem really is gigantic
Especially if we decide to panic.
That's enough now of this torment
Forget Christmas, it's more like Lent.

It's Christmas 2021 and rumours of shortages are rife.

Christmas Is Coming

Christmas is coming and the goose is getting fat,
Please put a tenner in the old man's hat.
He can't afford the heating and his house is very cold.
There's ice upon his windows and the walls are streaked with mould.

Christmas is coming and the goose is getting fat,
The only warm place round here is the local laundromat.
Everybody's frozen stiff with chilblains on their toes
And can't afford the tissues on which to wipe their nose.

Christmas is coming and the fat goose still expands,
We won't be able to pluck it, we have frostbite on our hands.
No one can play the grand piano any more,
We've chopped it up for firewood along with the front door.

Christmas is coming and the goose has disappeared,
Tipped off by some turkeys who had also been hand reared.
It seems they're in collusion and now they're on the run
We'll have a veggie Christmas. Now won't that be fun?

It's Christmas 2022 and things are no better.

Happy Christmas Everyone

Happy Christmas everyone!
You know those cards you sent?
They're heaped up in a corner
Getting damp and bent.

Happy Christmas everyone!
No, you can't go home by train
The drivers are pleading poverty
And you're part of their campaign.

Happy Christmas everyone!
The nurses have walked out
It's no good feeling poorly
Try not to pass out.

Happy Christmas everyone!
Be careful not to fall
Paramedics will not help you
However hard you call.

Happy Christmas everyone!
Go mad and have a blast.
The way the world is going
It could well be our last.

It's peace on Earth and goodwill etc. as the Royal Mail, railway workers, nurses and ambulance staff decide to strike.

Special Delivery!

It's a funny old business is Christmas,
When kids must appease Santa Claus,
Who squeezes himself down their chimneys
Drinking sherry as he loudly guffaws.

Tipsy from millions of schooners
All drunk in the space of one night,
Santa staggers about in the darkness
While striving to stay bolt upright.

He lurches and trips to the kitchen,
Helps himself to another mince pie
While Rudolph chomps on a carrot
As he gives Father Christmas the eye.

The deer knows when the sherry takes over,
And Santa can no longer stand,
He must carry him back to the North Pole
And tell him his sleigh has been banned.

And who will leave gifts for the children
At this magical Wonderland time?
There's only one likely contender,
Happy Christmas from Amazon Prime!

At Your Service

When setting out to serve the ball,
Some rules must be obeyed.
Otherwise you'll get called out
And lose points I'm afraid.

A big mistake some players make
Is to serve straight from their hand.
This is clearly out of order and
The practice should be banned.

You cannot hide the ball away
It must be plain to see
Balance it on your open palm
Then toss it vertically.

Sixteen centimetres is the height
That you should throw the ball.
Make sure you stand behind the line
And wait for it to fall.

Once the ball has left your hand,
You must not obscure its flight
As it bounces once then clears the net
To bounce the other side.

But should it touch the net en route
You can then call a let.
Go through the serve routine again
And go on to fight the set.

Once you've got the basics right,
You can fine tune some good serves,
Impart some calculated spin
Producing fiendish swerves.

So if you value honesty
And take pride in your name,
Remember to serve legally
And play a decent game.

This poem gives clear instructions on how to serve legally when playing table tennis. There's nothing like an illegal serve for winding people up.

Doh!

There's some kind of affliction
That seems to strike us all,
If you listen you will hear it
It's the table tennis player's call.

In doubles and in singles,
It happens just the same
It brings things to a halt
And interrupts the game.

It's the eternal question
You've heard countless times before
Up goes that old refrain,
I'm sorry, what's the score?

We've only played two minutes
And already minds are blank
Everyone's bewildered
It's a worry, let's be frank.

There follows much discussion
As everyone back tracks
And tries hard to remember
What exactly were the facts?

As the players seek agreement
Diplomacy prevails
And the score is fabricated
Before the game derails.

I don't know what the answer is
It's hard to get a grip
When one's faint hold on reality
Keeps giving you the slip.

Bojo

What's the matter Mr Johnson, you're looking rather glum?
Things are going badly and I'm sure there's worse to come.
You've been playing lots of games; you've broken all the rules.
Did you think we wouldn't notice? Do you take us all for fools?

We all get so exasperated Boris never learns.
He will insist on fiddling while the Tory party burns
He's his own worst enemy, of that you can be sure.
A lot of people say they don't trust him anymore.

We suggest his New Year resolution should be to tone it down,
Behave more like a statesman, not play up like a clown.
He should get his act together, listen more to us, not less
Because he's in danger of becoming a genuine Eton mess!!

Go Bojo, Go!

Never mind that Mr Putin's being such a pain,
Amassing all his troops, his eyes set on Ukraine.
Boris has been caught red-handed eating birthday cake!
A crime so dire the Met's been called in to investigate.

The allegations fly about whipped up by mischief makers
In the world of politics - no givers, only takers
Sorry Boris, looks as though you've blown out all your candles
Your legacy will be a mix of crumbs and social scandals.

Partygate

It seems that some in Downing Street
Have been a little indiscreet.
Their high jinks have now come to light.
The people say it isn't right.

It's caused a vast amount of fuss,
There's nothing else to be discussed.
The media becomes obsessed
And the PM is pursued with zest.

Meanwhile, waiting in the wings,
Dominic's busy pulling strings.
He's got photos, books and tapes,
Proof of BJ's jolly japes.

He adds more poison to the mess,
Drip feeds it to the waiting press
Who gulp it eagerly like Smarties
Handed out at children's parties.

Bent on mischief he holds proof
Of gatherings that will raise the roof.
He knows he won't be satisfied
'Til he's seen Boris crucified.

Once best friends, now daggers drawn,
Hell hath no fury like Cummings scorned.
Boris must be made to pay
And will, if Mad Dom gets his way.

To be continued ...

Guilty as Charged

"I was only there nine minutes, and no cake passed my lips."
Says Boris in defence as widespread consternation grips.
"Sorry Mr Johnson, you can bluster all day long,
But what you did was stupid and undeniably wrong.
Now you've been found guilty of breaking your own law,
So stump up fifty quid – no doubt there will be more.
What's it going to take to make you toe the line?
Considerably more than a paltry little fine."

Meanwhile Putin puts the boot in and Zelensky blows up tanks
While beseeching that he needs aid from the British and the Yanks.
If it wasn't quite so awful, it would really make you laugh
That our PM's been caught partying with a handful of his staff.
The opposition love it now they can hurl their just abuse.
They've got him where they want him, his head is in the noose.
And all the while in Ukraine they're blown to Kingdom come
For standing by their principles and their refusal to succumb.

Hasta la Vista, Baby!

Boris, you've really let me down,
Once too often messed around.
Your downfall comes as no surprise
You're not averse to telling lies.
You've never really quite grown up,
You're something of a playful pup
But everybody's had enough
And they've decided to get tough.

I for one will miss your pranks,
For which I give you grateful thanks.
I've lost count of the many times
You gave me fodder for my rhymes.
Now I must look to someone new
Who won't be off the wall like you
In future everyone will say,
He was the one who got away.

Hasta la vista, baby!

No, life isn't the same without Boris. He may be impetuous and careless, but he is rarely boring.

Piracy Diplomacy

Watch out for Monsieur Macron,
As slippery as an eel,
He has plans to sink the English
And applies himself with zeal.

He wants revenge for Brexit,
He's feeling rather shirty
And, typical of a Frenchman,
He's prepared to play it dirty.

He strides onto the world stage,
A smile fixed upon his face.
He's intent on blackmail,
He's an absolute disgrace.

He likes to flex his muscles,
Fistbumps Boris with French flair
While he plans to wreck our future
(Surely not? He would not dare!)

Boris Johnson humphs and stutters,
Puts the Navy under orders
To look out for French pirates
As it patrols our borders.

He says Macron's a fool
Who likes to swipe at our morale.
We give a Gallic shrug and say
Good bye entente cordial.

Matt Finish

Matt Hancock went and blew it,
Now he must pay the price.
His wife is really livid
And says he's not been nice.

Old Cummings thinks it's funny –
What else did we expect?
He told us Matt was rubbish,
It seems he was correct.

While we were all in lockdown
Did what we'd been told,
Matt was snogging Gina
With a passion uncontrolled.

He gave in to temptation,
Got completely swept away,
Borne up on primal urges
Forgot he'd have to pay.

It's the Westminster pandemic,
It's been around for years.
It strikes down politicians
And can terminate careers.

The alpha male variant,
As it is widely known,
Strikes behind closed doors
Its origins unknown.

Its victims rendered breathless,
Blood pressure through the roof
Protesting at their innocence
They thought they were bullet proof.

So, Matt's keeping a low profile
Until the fuss dies down
And people's fickle memories
Give him back his crown.

Who would have thought that Mr Hancock would go on to create even more of a stir when he appeared in I'm a Celebrity, Get Me Out of Here! I'll say no more.

Mr and Mrs Dishy Rishi

Now he's making headlines, as is his lady wife.
His foes are out to get him; they plan to twist the knife.
This rich and glamorous couple are seen to be fair game
They'll have their work cut out trying to defend their name.
Anyone who is lucky to have lots and lots of dosh,
Triggers great resentment and especially if they're posh.
Now it seems that Rishi is not so squeaky clean
(Though frankly he's not the worst offender that there's ever been.)
Can he ride out the controversy until his enemies tire
Or should he slink away before he sinks into the mire?

To be continued ...

PM

Then there's the Prime Minister,
As fair as Rishi's dark.
Disillusioned with the job -
He only took it for a lark.

He shouted loud for Brexit,
Whipped up a noisy storm.
Never dreamt that death and illness
Would soon become the norm.

Fate hangs heavy on his shoulders,
The situation's getting tough.
Bluff and bluster are his trademark
He hadn't planned for all this stuff.

Covid-19 tried to kill him,
Laid him very low in bed
Does he ever rue recovering?
Sometimes wish that he was dead?

Now he has a poisoned chalice
From which he has to sip.
While the whole world faces ruin
And chaos has us in its grip.

Good Luck Liz

Atta girl, go get 'em! Give them all what for!
Surround yourself with competence and show your foes the door.
You've got no time to mess around, the eleventh hour is here
The sands of time are running low and soon they'll disappear.

The Opposition will try and fool you and hope to make you trip
And some of your back benchers would like to see you slip,
But you must rise above them and see the way ahead,
Despite attacks from trolls and those who'd rather see you dead.

Focus on your targets, find the country's sharpest minds,
Bring the experts all together, be prepared to take all kinds.
You may not have the answers, but your job is to inspire
And lead when things are desperate and the country's under fire.

So don your navy two piece, put family life on hold
While you show the rest of Europe that now we must be bold.
Stand firmly with our allies and speak with one clear voice,
Then all the world will know that you were the perfect choice.

Part Two

I think we know the answer,
It's plain for all to see –
Liz, she went and blew it
Her dream was not to be.

Her life is now in boxes,
She'd only just moved in
And now she's moved back out again
It seems she just can't win.

Just when you think things can't get any worse, …

Not So Great Britain

Britain is no longer Great
We've lost our way, we're in a state
For months now we've been flying blind
While values have been undermined.

Our politicians weep and wail
They've put the country up for sale
We're in a tailspin, going down
Very soon we'll hit the ground.

There's no time to think things through
Our leaders don't know what to do
Sound bites cannot help us now
We need to get a grip somehow .

We cannot see, the light grows dim
The situation's really grim
There is no one left to trust
They've had to sack dear Lizzie Truss.

So who will now take up the reins
Have we anyone with brains?
Oh look, it's Rishi, he's the man
Surely he must have a plan?

But we're distracted by his suit
Which makes him look quite coy and cute
His tailoring is quite deficient
His trouser length is insufficient.

And all the while the prices rise
Inflation's at an all-time high.
Nobody knows what they're doing
We're on the road to rack and ruin.

I'm sorry, but it's difficult to maintain one's levels of optimism.

Bon Voyage

I'm on a cruise to nowhere,
Going to take it nice and slow,
Let myself be pampered,
Feel all my tension go.

I'll have breakfast in my cabin
A little after nine.
No need to get up early -
That will suit me fine.

I might glance through the papers
As I choose something for dinner.
The vegetarian option
Looks like it'll be a winner.

In between my meals
When there's nothing much to do,
I'll relax and put my feet up
On board the QE2.

When the trip is over
And our sailing days are done,
I'll be glad I made the effort,
It was time I had some fun.

I wrote this for my godmother who was looking forward to going away after the pandemic.

Sports Day

They're under starter's orders,
They're champing at the bit
They've done some high intensity training
They're feeling pretty fit.

Some limber up with stretches
Some jog upon the spot
Others use deep breathing
To show what poise they've got.

For weeks they all have practiced
One eye upon the clock
Shaving off the seconds
As they leave the starting block.

Now here is the race
They've waited for all year
They've splashed out on new trainers
And the designer gear.

And now, at last, they're off
At quite a frantic pace
Reputations are at stake
In the annual parents' race.

Olly's mum's the first to trip
And she crashes to the ground
Her arms are flailing wildly
As she brings three others down.

Meanwhile dads are doing battle
They know their pride's at stake
Jostling for position
They try to overtake

In minutes it's all over
Most have paid a price
Two have sprained an ankle
And are calling for some ice.

Everyone is limping
Someone's got a cough
Another's burst a blister
And the skin is hanging off.

The children are on standby
And give them all a cheer
Then steer their parents home
They'll try again next year.

It's Not Funny (or Clever)

When was the last time
a comedian made you roar
Until you begged for mercy
Crying, "stop, stop! No more!"?

It hasn't happened lately
Of that there is no doubt
Because wit and entertainment
Have been axed and elbowed out.

We're bombarded by the f word
Or very often worse
It really isn't funny
Hearing people curse.

The men are truly awful
The women just as bad
They shout and hurl expletives
They sound completely mad.

Where are the sharp one liners?
The sort that makes you choke
These days it's all so boring
Can no one tell a joke?

There's little skill in shouting
Which has become a craze
While pandering to wokes
Who rule the roost these days

Apparently good humour
Is nowhere to be found
The politically correct lot
Have pushed it underground.

Alf Garnett and Les Dawson
Would be run out of town
Or charged with inciting hatred
And summarily sent down.

So where will we find laughter
That makes us gasp and scream?
It's lost and gone forever
Now we can only dream.

Rebellious octogenarians now huddle covertly in groups recalling the politically incorrect Carry On films of the last century.

Remotely Controlled

I'm sitting in front of the telly,
Trying to think what to do.
Remote control at my disposal,
I'm trying to think it all through.

My brain takes one look and it freezes,
It sulks and gets into a strop,
Very quickly runs out of patience
And shouts 'just make it stop!'

How can you call all this progress?
I feel that I need a degree.
Or maybe I should be certified,
Cos it all seems a bit crazy to me.

A router should live in the garden,
A menu says what you can eat,
And buttons are what keep your clothes on
Or given to tots as a treat!

I'm just looking for some amusement,
Something to while away time.
Maybe some comic nostalgia,
But this is a mountain to climb.

Oh that we could go backwards
Forget this technology craze
When life was so very much simpler
I still hanker after those days.

I must pull myself back together
I mustn't let my mind roam
I remember one thing to do quite clearly
When lost, I need to press 'home'

Now look, this is just what I needed,
Here's something that's called a guide.
I'll press that and see what might happen
At least I can say that I tried.

D'you know, I think if I practice,
I'll eventually be able to cope.
I'll whizz quickly round all the channels
I'm not, after all, such a dope!

Dad had bought a new TV package and was receiving instruction from my husband (aka Gadget Man and subject of the next poem).

Gadget Man

Gadget man's alive and well and living here with me.
I'm a confirmed luddite and so last century.
He's into online shopping and surfs the net each day
Looking at the latest trends on Amazon and eBay.

The house is full of cables which drive me round the bend,
They'd stretch around the planet if laid end to end
And now they're all redundant and when I enquire why,
Cos everything's gone wireless with the advent of WiFi.

He's got an app for everything, they help him run his life.
The only disadvantage is, they all confuse his wife!
The lighting changes colour, it now comes in various hues,
But as far as I'm concerned, it just gives me the blues.

So all you crazy scientists, stop inventing stuff
Because as far as I'm concerned, we've got more than enough!
Life's become more complex than it needs to be,
Let's shake off these gadgets and let ourselves run free.

The years steadily pass and few of us seem to change much. Gerry has been trying to coach me in basic IT skills for 20 years. I admire his persistence, but results are very sketchy.

A Waiter's Tale

Now look here boss, it's just not right
To keep us waiting half the night.
Those women thought they owned the place
They should be pinged by track and trace.
All they did was drink and talk.
I wanted them to take a walk.
I'm not trying to be funny
And I know you need their money
They didn't leave til nearly ten
I wanted to be home by then
I'm not used to working late
When other punters leave at eight.
If they book again, think hard
And tell them that they are now barred
That will teach them all to hurry
The next time that they want a curry.

My friends and I were so glad to finally meet together after the lockdowns, we couldn't stop talking despite being the last people in the Indian restaurant. One waiter in particular became very agitated at our reluctance to leave.

Bonkers

Listen up people. The world has gone mad.
We all hated the lockdowns and thought they were bad.
We wanted them lifted so we could be free,
We wanted our lives back how they used to be.

Now just weeks later things have turned manic
Cos someone said "there's no petrol! Don't panic!"
Now we all queue and get into a strop
Can no one see this behaviour must stop?

One day we're told that the shelves will be bare,
That Christmas will be a no-turkey affair.
Rumours abound that there'll be no more gas –
Somebody needs a good kick up the ass.

Please would someone demonstrate quiet restraint
When wanting to kick off and make a complaint
And rather than witness the worst side of life,
Can we try to stay calm and put down the knife.

Cos really, quite frankly, it has to be said
The proportion of idiots seems quite widespread.
If you really must know who and what are to blame,
It can only be us to our crying shame.

Hang on a Minute

"You are currently caller number fifteen in the queue"
So now I must decide what I want to do -
Hang on for all eternity 'til my patience peters out
Listening to piped music before I scream and shout.

"You are currently caller number thirteen in the queue"
This is going to take an age, I think I'll make a brew
Waiting rooms have long since closed, the chairs no longer there
I have the distinct impression that no one seems to care.

"You are currently caller number eleven in the queue"
I could really do without all this mindless ballyhoo.
What about the Hippocratic oath that says you can't play god?
The refusal to see patients strikes me as very odd.

"You are currently caller number nine in the queue"
I rage and swear and curse like mad, the air itself turns blue.
I've not seen nurse or doctor for very many years
Not since they outsourced everything, like syringing of blocked ears.

"You are currently caller number eight in the queue"
My patience is now running out and I think I need the loo
Once the pride of British life, the NHS is sinking fast
I hate to have to say it but the people now come last.

"You are currently caller number five in the queue"
What on earth is happening, what do the doctors do?
Are they playing indoor golf? Reading War and Peace?
Putting a deposit on a holiday in Greece?

"You are currently caller number two in the queue"
I'm very nearly there now, I shall see this torment through.
Then suddenly I hear a voice. Thank goodness, cos it's late.
"Ring back tomorrow caller, the line opens again at eight."

As soon as I say the first line to a live audience, there's a ripple of recognition as people recall similar unhelpful experiences.

Dressing Down

The biggest challenge of the day
Is getting dressed - once child's play.
I don't know which garment's worst
If you ask me, each one is cursed.

Pants are where the nightmare starts
And my sanity soon departs.
Feeble hands clutch tight elastic
A miracle now would be fantastic.

Nothing gets me more depressed
Than wrestling with my wretched vest.
And when I finally get it on,
I can feel I've got it wrong.

The whole thing now is front to back
I'm at great risk of heart attack.
The entire procedure takes an age
And soon I start to rant and rage.

I simply want to tuck it in
But, it seems I cannot win.
My despair is quite profound
I don't have time to mess around.

Socks and shoes. Need I say more?
You and I both know the score.
I try to bend down to my feet,
But sense the onset of defeat.

The time has come to make a stand.
I hope that you will understand.
I don't intend to cause a sensation,
But I've joined the Naturist Foundation.

And as everybody knows,
Members there dispense with clothes.
Nudity is not a sin,
I know that I will fit right in.

After the best part of seventy years dressing and undressing at the drop of a hat, suddenly I can't do it anymore. It's crazy. It's also infuriating because I can no longer wear what I like, only what I can get on.

Who Cares?

Were you taught to go the extra mile all those years ago
When you were swotting up on what there was to know?
Did your tutors teach compassion and what caring really means?
Was empathy a quality they encouraged behind the scenes?
No. I suspect that you're self-taught and not afraid to give yourself,
It's packets, pills and potions that stay safe upon the shelf.

You understand your patients, you know what makes them tick,
There are very many reasons why a person may feel sick.
To make someone feel better, you treat the body, mind and soul.
For a cure to be effective, you see the person as a whole.
Your thoughtful added extras help your clients sleep at night
Keep doing what you do Louise, because you do it all just right.

Louise, the Community Matron, who keeps an eye on my father now that he's on his own, continues to provide patients and their families with care and support. I don't know what we'd do without her.

Be Careful

Be careful on the stairs Mum,
Make sure you hold the rail.
You've reached that sort of age when
You're starting to get frail.

While we're on the subject,
Don't climb up on the stools
And do you think it's wise
To walk around in mules?

You've got to be more cautious,
You can't just rush about.
Who will pick you up
If you trip and get knocked out?

Perhaps you should stop gardening
And read a book instead
And ditch that racing bike of yours
Before it kills you dead.

No, I'm not a killjoy
And, yes, you must have fun,
I only want what's best for you
When all is said and done.

Whatever do you mean Mum?
You've sold your house and car?
Are you moving to a nice flat
Where you won't need to walk far?

What's that you say? Who's Carlos?
Didn't he teach you how to dance?
You're starting a joint venture soon
In the south of France!!!

This was inspired by a recently widowed friend whose children were panicking over her living alone. But as we all know, despite any frailties, we are all aged 21 at heart and will continue to do naughty things like clambering up on the furniture when no one's looking.

You What?

There's a very common ailment
That strikes at married life.
It affects both men and women
Causing untold strife.

Difficult to diagnose
Until it's well engrained,
It can cause a lot of shouting
While expressions become pained.

The chances are you've got it
And have had it for a while
If you show the following symptoms
And conversation is a trial.

He says you talk too softly
That you sound more like a mouse.
You say he's out of earshot
Speaking from the far end of the house.

You say he's always grunting,
That his favourite word is 'eh'
He sounds like he's not bothered,
So you take it the wrong way.

And neither of you notice
That the TV volume's high
And the world is very quiet
But you don't think to ask why.

In growing old together
You've also become deaf.
Of mutual understanding,
There's very little left.

How can you restore the harmony
You knew in yester-year
When you whispered such sweet nothings
In your darling's shell-like ear?

Perhaps now the time has come
To let go of your pride
Fit those digital hearing aids
And lead your lives AMPLIFIED!!!!

At the time of writing, there are just another three weeks until I go for my hearing test. I'm fed up with not being able to follow films or jokes and I'm discovering how isolating it is to always be on the outside when in a group situation. If you recognise this scenario, I urge you to do likewise.

Boy to Man

When I was born a baby
In nineteen twenty eight,
Life was pretty basic
Just enough food on my plate.
Making do and mending
Were the order of the day
And when I'd done my chores
I would run outside and play.

Our toys were rough and ready
And we only had a few,
But I'd lark about the fields
With a few boys that I knew.
And while the war was raging,
We took it in our stride
Went scrumping in the orchards,
Made dens in which to hide.

Fast forward eighty years or more
The world's a different place
Full of noise and bustle
And I struggle to keep pace.
Men have conquered Everest
And landed on the moon
While I battle with the time
And wonder why it's gone so soon.

I look back at those bygone days
And remember how it felt
Racketing down the lanes
As I rode my bike full pelt.
With no thought of the future
And the man I'd come to be
Never dreaming for a minute
That I'd reach ninety three!

Happy Birthday Dad!!!!!

All Washed Up

The washing up's a nuisance
That I've come to dread.
I'd rather put my feet up
And have a kip instead.

I really don't want the bother
Of using pots and pans,
So now I pay attention to
My daily mealtime plans.

Fish and chips on Fridays
Produces cutlery and plate.
The only disadvantage is
That baking tin I hate.

Wiltshire Farm at weekends
Come in a plastic tray.
I throw them when I finish
So that suits me ok.

I've recently discovered,
And it's something of a scoop,
For just three bits of washing up
I can open Heinz Big Soup.

So if you want to visit,
Do what my daughter's do -
Come and do the cooking
Then clear and wash up too.

Of all the chores that Dad now has to do, I think it's washing up that he hates the most.

The Other Woman

Shame on anyone who dares
To compare me with Pam Ayres!
People do it all the time
Every time I spout a rhyme.

I'm told I sound a lot like her
With my rural sounding burr,
But let me make it very plain
The two of us are not the same.

Yes, I know she did it first
And in her trade she is well versed.
I only started for a lark
But now I want to make my mark.

At her age she should be retired,
I'm the one who should be hired
Because, you know, I'm nice and cheap
Her ticket price will make you weep.

Her hardback books upon display
Are very good, but you will pay.
Her dental bill is causing grief – well,
She should have looked after her teeth!

I feel I can compete with Pam on an equal footing until it comes to performing. I don't know a single rhyme off by heart and therefore I have to read everything. Still, I can blame it on the Parkinson's.

Cake

The ultimate in comfort food
Is a moist, cream filled cake
Baked by a WI expert,
It's bliss for Heaven's sake!

Oh go on then, just a small slice,
I can't resist the taste
Even though the blasted thing
plays havoc with my waist.

Shall I finish up this scone
Before the cream goes off?
I'll just add a touch more jam
If it's dry it'll make me cough!

Is that the last eclair?
Don't leave it on the plate
I expect you want to wash up
As it's getting a bit late.

And what about that bun?
What a shame if it went stale.
I'll pop it in my hand bag,
No wonder diets always fail!

My favourite's lemon drizzle -
Is there any left?
Oh no, it's all been eaten
And now I feel bereft.

What true culinary delights
You cooks know how to make.
Marie Antoinette knew what she was doing
When she told us to eat cake.

Crumbs

Consider now the humble cake
And the difference it can make
It comforts you when you are down
And has been known to smooth a frown.
Eat it when you entertain
Just sniffing one will keep you sane.
Share a carrot cake with friends
Its soothing quality never ends.
As a bribe they work well too
I'd do anything, wouldn't you?
And here's a final useful trick
You can use a stale one as a brick.

What's Brewing?

I remember tramping the hedgerows
Looking for any tell-tale sign
Of the much maligned Sambucus,
Our own particular vine.

Despised by lots of gardeners
As an unwanted and overgrown weed,
The elder offered us treasure
For which we were grateful indeed.

Its flowers must be picked in the sunshine
And steeped to draw their perfume.
A jugful of elderflower blossom
Will gradually pervade the whole room.

Then, by some magical process
Involving some sugar and yeast,
The mixture becomes an elixir
Champagne to grace any feast.

We took great care not to be greedy
Not to strip all the flowers away
But leave some to grow into berries
For they will make red wine some day.

This innocent powerful home brew
Would ease aching joints, said our nan
At which we would all raise our glasses
And down it in one to a man.

Both my grandmother and then my mother, went in for brewing vast quantities of country wines, and by far and away the most popular, was the elderflower.

Halloween

Ghosts and ghouls and zombies
And things that go bump in the night.
Let's terrorise our small children
And give them all a big fright.

The rest of the year we protect them
And keep them away from all harm.
Until one dark night in October
When we fill them with fear and alarm.

We dress up in dark rags and tatters,
Take them out under cover of night,
Creeping around in the damp streets.
How can that ever be right?

We knock on the doors of strangers,
We haven't a clue who they are.
We say it's ok to take sweeties
Don't you think this behaviour's bizarre?

Let's scrap this American custom
And look to our own British ways.
Like burning effigies of Guy Fawkes
While the kids dance with glee at the blaze.

When the Balloon Goes Up

When the balloon goes up, as one day it will do
I shall not be found wanting because I've thought it through
I know I can survive without the luxury of power
I could build a shelter or rig up an outdoor shower.

You might know how to download and print out a couple of files
But could you lay a hedge or replace cracked ceiling tiles?
People in this day and age have very little clue
How to live a simple life or know how to make do.

Our lives become more complex with every passing day
Everything's connected but in a complicated way
A PHD in IT is what you need today
But I refuse to give in and throw my pen away.

When some great disaster befalls our planet earth
You'll wish you'd paid attention to the things that keep their worth
Like knowing how to light a lamp instead of flick a switch
Or which leaves will soothe your skin when the nettles make it itch.

Ok, I'm an eccentric, you may think my views are daft
But with the world that's fast unravelling, I may have the last laugh.
So stock up on some tins of beans and piles of Oxo cubes
Then you won't be caught napping when we all go down the tubes!

Gloom

Try turning off the TV and the radio too
Cancel all the papers - cos they're no good for you.
Mother Earth's in uproar and all the news is bad
Dwelling on the negatives is driving people mad.
The future looks precarious, full of fear and threat
While each passing year has been the scariest yet

Global warming says the ice will melt and sea levels will rise
As the smoke from a million bush fires drifts across the skies
Animals of all kinds will struggle to survive
As habitats disappear, they can no longer thrive
No one is responsible and no one seems to care
Populations keep on growing though there's hardly room to spare.

We're hellbent on destruction and cannot change our ways
We live only for the present, but we're in a terminal phase
Future generations must take pot luck and keep their fingers crossed
As we approach the point of no return and our way of life is lost
Let's bury our heads deep in the sand, like we've always done
We may have wrecked the planet, but boy, we've had some fun.

Adverse Adverts

Can you make sense of the adverts
Beamed into our homes every day?
I find it almost impossible to
Work out what they're trying to say
One minute I'm looking at meerkats
Doing all sorts of ridiculous things,
Then staff are ice skating in Asda
While a beefburger quietly sings.

But there's a careful use of ethnicities
You don't have to look very hard
At whatever is being marketed
To see all-white ads are now barred.
John Smith and his two point four children,
Who live in the suburbs of Reading,
Have suddenly lost their identity
And wonder where the future is heading.

The pendulum just keeps on swinging
First one way then to the other.
After day comes inevitable night,
From one extreme to another.
We can't seem to halt these sea changes
Even if they're not fair or not right.
We all jump to our own conclusions
For goodness sake can't we unite?

The Handcart

We're off to hell in a handcart,
Hop on and take your place.
There's room enough for everyone
In this wacky crazy race.

Jump aboard you scammers,
Always trying to fleece the poor,
And you woke enthusiasts
Free speech is no more.

Warmongers and rapists,
There's plenty of room for you.
Knife wielders, and groomers,
Justice is long overdue.

I can squeeze in a couple of conmen
And those who peddle drugs,
Abetted by their henchmen
Who are nothing more than thugs.

Now you're all together,
Here's a bit of luck -
In another seven seconds
This cart will self D-E-S-T-R-U-C-T   .... !

The pen is mightier than the sword.   I've discovered I can make anything happen in the world of Liz.

Perfect Storm

We've come through the pandemic
And now there's global drought
Except for those with flash floods
Whose lives have been washed out.

Fish are dying in the shallows,
The grass has turned to straw
Tinder for the wild fires
That race across the moors.

Soggy British summers
Have vanished clean away
Vaporised by heat waves
That leave us parched each day.

There's talk of mass starvation
As crops shrivel up and die
This wasn't meant to happen
Now we're asking why?

We're a civilised society
Our intelligence is vast
But in the world of common sense
We're definitely last.

We've lived beyond our means
The planet's been stripped bare
We've made no provision for tomorrow
Because no one thought to care

Civilisation has unravelled
There is no going back
Our former way of life
Is now under attack.

A new life now awaits us
We must be strong and brave
Or else we're doomed to failure
With nothing left to save.

'm beginning to sound like the old soothsayer in the 1970s sitcom 'Up Pompei' who used to wander about intoning 'Woe. Woe. And thrice woe.'

Modern Living

We've opened up the chimney
And now we're burning sticks.
We can't afford gas heating
So now we're in a fix.

I've had to join the food bank,
For which there's now a queue.
People are in crisis
And don't know what to do.

The world's gone into free fall,
There seem to be no rules.
Nations now are led
By despots, thugs and fools.

Sects and factions prosper,
Their policies absurd,
But this is how it is now -
Welcome to our world!

Progress has skidded to an abrupt halt and now we seem to be going backwards.

Tighten Your Belts

The price of bread has rocketed
And so has Wiltshire ham.
Sunday roast's a distant dream,
We're lucky to have spam.

Shortages are common
We're going back in time
When food was treated with respect
And gluttony was a crime.

Now fridges are half empty,
Mary Berry's born again
As she shows us how to manage
When there is no quiche Lorraine.

Take aways have vanished
As have buy one, get one free
There are no more special offers
And there's nothing much for tea.

Tomorrow's jam's been eaten,
Weve gobbled all the cake.
There's only bread, no butter
Our ice cream's lost its flake.

It's time to settle up now
Your tab has reached the end.
Please don't ask for credit
As a refusal may offend.

Cooee!!!!

Hey there, just a minute!
Why not take a look
At something a bit different
'Tween the covers of this book.

I've written bits of nonsense
To entertain and tease,
As well as raise some money
For those with Parkinson's Disease.

A neurological disorder
That isn't very nice,
It affects a lot of people
Who pay a heavy price.

You can offer your support,
As well as have a laugh,
When you buy my book of rhymes,
Most of which are pretty daft.

One of my sales posters advertising my books. All the money I raise through book sales and poetry recitals goes to Parkinsons Table Tennis.

Sixty Not Out

Time was, when you reached sixty
You could stop work and retire,
But someone moved the goalposts
And you find you're still for hire.

Condemned to keep on working
Forever and a day,
Retirement's but a dream
And still so far away.

So now, instead of lazing
And taking life real slow,
You've got to soldier onwards
And be forever on the go.

So while I'm having lunch
At a nice country retreat,
I'll remember that you're absent
And reserve an empty seat.

And when the waiter's filled my glass
With a dry white chilled house wine
I shall drink a toast to Gaynor
Who should be here with me, to dine ....

In recent years we women have had the retirement pension age to deal with. Most of us have had to lose out on thousands of pounds worth of pension and work far longer than we ever expected.

Number Three

Is it really happening? Surely it can't be
That I'm already writing poems for volume number three?

Book two was published yesterday and I thought I'd have a rest
Yet here I am still musing over which words rhyme the best.

I know it won't be easy to go to print three times,
But I think that I will call it something like 'A Life of Rhymes'

And as regards the topics, I don't yet have a plan
I'll wait and see what turns up then describe it if I can.

I know the politicians will provide me with a feast
Of careless indiscretions , I can rely on them at least.

We'll also get to see how the pandemic settles down
As it becomes part of the fabric in each and every town.

There'll be the usual family things that happen to us all
The rest is speculation - I don't have a crystal ball.

Meanwhile I must get on with marketing and make sure people look
Or else why am I writing yet another silly book?

This seemed to literally jump out of the end of my pen.

Supermarket Checkout

I get to the checkout and reach for my purse.
I can't find it of course and silently curse.
How hard can it be to pay up and go?
Why am I now so impossibly slow?

Aware that people behind me are starting to queue,
I upend my bag and start to hunt through.
There are too many pockets, too many folds,
My hesitant fingers won't do what they're told.

Lots of compartments that serve to confuse
This is all part of the shopping day blues.
At last I am done and can't wait to get out,
But I hear a loud noise and somebody shouts.

It seems I've set off the blasted alarm!
But it wasn't me, I've done them no harm.
I have to wait while my shopping is viewed
Personally I think it's terribly rude.

And as it turns out it's their fault, not mine.
They've left the tag on a bottle of wine
And now I blush red as if I'm accused
Of drinking too much and they're all amused.

The way that I trip and stumble and sway,
They obviously think I indulge every day.
I think for a mo should I try to explain?
But decide in the end that there's nothing to gain.

And so I lurch home, not sure what to think,
But one thing's for sure - Parkinson's stinks!

I used to quite like shopping, but things seem to happen to me on every excursion now, no matter how hard I try and prepare.

God Save the Queen

I've outstayed most world leaders
And hung onto my crown.
I've always done my duty,
I've never let you down.

My attention span is awesome
And I know how to behave.
My manners are classed as top drawer
As I gently nod and wave.

I'm running out of time now
As my reign comes to a close.
Time to pass the sceptre
To another I suppose.

I've always kept my counsel,
My opinions under wraps.
Monarchy needs mystery
To keep it from collapse.
.
I've had one or two issues
That have brought some pangs of grief.
Harry's been a nuisance,
And Andrew's beyond belief!

After all these years of service,
All I seek now is peace.
An eternity of freedom
Will be a great release.

I wrote this for the Queen's Jubilee.

QE2 RIP

Perched upon this catafalque for everyone to see,
It'll be a few days yet until I'm finally set free.
This is my last hurrah, grand finale, one more goodbye
Then you must put your grief aside and here's the reason why.
You've stood in line for countless hours, sometimes cold and wet'
Quietly contemplating life as you pay me your respects.
The winning formula for peace, or so it seems to me,
Commit to serving others and be the best that you can be.
Now lay me to rest, commit my body to the ground
And let my soul soar free, no longer duty bound.
I'll saddle up my winged horse and together we'll take flight
And you might see a shooting star one clear and frosty night.

Part 2

The International Collection

Belonging to the PPP family has made a substantial change to my life. So far, I've competed in Germany, Portugal and Croatia. I have friends from around the world and I've been adopted as the official PPP poet. Little did I dream during the lockdown days that life would become so interesting.

Now read the next batch of rhymes which are a blend of table tennis and Parkinson's.

PingPongParkinsons
Table Tennis Tournaments

German Open, Nordhorn September 2021………….. 60

World Championships, Berlin, September 2021……. 68

German Open, Bad Homburg, May, 2022………........ 78

Portuguese Open, Estoril, June, 2022……………........ 84

World Championships, Pula, Croatia, October, 2022. 90

German Open, Nordhorn September 2021

Afternoon Tea 61
Called Up 62
Pride of England.............................. 63
Elite Athlete 64
Hilfe…………..…............................. 65
Heartbreak… 66
Martyn's Bag ……………...………… 67

Nordhorn saw me winning a silver medal with Martyn (from Wales) in the mixed doubles competition.

Afternoon Tea

What better way to raise some funds!
Let's eat some scones and currant buns.
Bara brith and short bread too
Go down lovely with a brew.
Oh good. I've spotted sausage plait -
I'd really like a piece of that
And what else is there to consume?
Mmm, lemon drizzle I presume.
Excuse me while I cut a slice
I love this stuff, it's very nice.
Focus only on the taste
Do not worry about your waist
Be sure to mop up every crumb
And add some padding to your bum

This relates to the first fundraising event to help players who wanted to compete in the Berlin, PingPongParkinson World Championships. The fundraiser was organised by my table tennis club and held at the home of one of its members. Imagine a table bearing all sorts of homemade cakes – gorgeous!

Called Up

It really is quite crazy,
I'm stunned beyond belief,
I've got to play for England
A career that will be brief.

Have I displayed great prowess?
Won every single game?
No, I've languished in the doldrums
And my shots are rather tame.

It's not for want of trying
I practice every day,
But my averages are lowly
And I guess that's how they'll stay.

So how come, at sixty seven
I realise a dream
To represent my country
And join a national team?

I'll let you know my secret
Even though I like to tease,
My extra special quality is
Parkinson's Disease!

These are indeed exciting times which sometimes felt quite bizarre.

Pride of England

Not normally one to wave a flag
And get all sentimental,
Indeed, I find too much of that
Can be quite detrimental.
But somehow, when I see those lions
Lying passant in a row,
I cannot help but feel inside
A patriotic glow.

And did those paws in ancient times
Stalk England's mountains green?
What battles and great conquests
Have those warriors seen?
Can I now conduct myself
In such a fitting manner
As to emulate these three brave beasts,
Fight well beneath their banner?

Whichever way you look at it
Win or lose is much the same.
It's not just racking up the points
It's how you play the game.
Can you smile and face adversity,
Be generous in defeat?
Or will you whimper, whine and snivel
Cos someone has you beat?

So rouse yourselves, prepare to fight!
Let ENGLAND! be our cry
As we face the opposition
And prepare to do or die.
We'll give it everything we've got
And then we'll give some more
As we listen to King Harry's lions
Give out their mighty roar!

I was inspired to write this after spotting the three lions on our sports kit.

Elite Athlete

Now we're internationals,
Does it mean that we're elite?
Can we strut about a bit?
We're feeling quite upbeat.

We're sure to fail a drugs test
That much is guaranteed,
And we're all so used to freezing,
We don't usually do speed.

Will we be served much quicker
When we turn up at the bar?
Will people buy us drinks
And admire us from afar?

Will I switch on the Christmas lights
And then address the crowd?
Listen to the Mayor declare
"You've done the locals proud".

Apparently, international sports competitors are referred to as elite athletes. We found it hilarious to now find ourselves in that category.

Martyn's Bag

Martyn's bag is deadly
He can't leave it alone.
It's full of bits and pieces
And weighs about two stone.

He carts it down to breakfast
And then back up the stairs.
We'd like to take it off him
But no one actually dares.

It's always in a muddle,
Full up with odds and ends
And a magnetic attraction
That only Martyn comprehends.

The mundane-looking backpack
Contains his heart and soul.
He'd be lost without it,
It's what keeps him whole.

There's something about bags and Parkinson's; they seem to take on Bermuda Triangle qualities. We know we've put our keys in a side pocket so that they are safe and secure, only to get into a panic later when they're nowhere to be found. After breaking into a sweat and causing some uproar, they are of course found sitting innocently in the side pocket where they've been all along. This is an almost daily event.

World Championships, Berlin, September 2021

Who am I.. 69
Ping Pong Parkinson Berlin.................. 70
United Front...................................... 71
Drawing a Blank 72
Our PD 73
Factotum ......…................................ 74
Top Man 75
Lizzie! Lizzie! Lizzie! 76
International..................................... 77

Who am I?

Standing here before you
I cut a sorry sight.
My shoulders hunching forwards,
My thin hair looks a fright.

My knees are stiff and creaky
And my hip has been replaced.
Of my former god-like body,
Not an atom can be traced.

An overactive bladder
Is the one thing that still works.
My hands are worse than useless
As I paw the air with jerks.

But I can still play ping pong
And make that small ball spin
Even with my Parkinson's,
Whatever shape I'm in.

And what has made me chuckle
As I wobble on my feet?
It's a bit late in the day but
I'm now an elite athlete!

PingPongParkinson Berlin

PingPongParkinson
All around the world.
Ping Pong Parkinson
The banner's now unfurled.
Ping Pong Parkinson
Nenad doffs his hat
Ping Pong Parkinson.
Time to wield your bat.
Ping Pong Parkinson
Daring to be bold
Ping Pong Parkinson
Taking home a gold.

This was the first time I met Nenad Bach properly, when he came and joined us Brits for team photos on our last celebratory evening in Berlin. In somewhat theatrical fashion I recited this short rhyme to him. This marked a major development in my poetry career as I was to find out in the coming weeks and months.

United Front

Andrew Cassy and his scouts come marching into town.
Fresh from the German Open where they threw their gauntlet down.

Here are the reinforcements come to swell the team
To sweep all before them as they realise their dream.

Prepared to take the battle to each and every foe
They will give no quarter as they lay opponents low.

So quake all you pretenders as you take fright and hide,
Because you're going to take a beating from Andrew Cassy's side.

Andrew, Martyn and I were joined in Berlin by reinforcements for the England side plus a contingent from Scotland. My intention was to write a rallying war cry to bind us together as we took on the rest of the world, but I think in the end it was seen more as a challenge between England and Scotland (Twickenham all over again).

Drawing a Blank

Behind this blank expression lies
A passionate heart of fire.
You see an empty vessel,
I'm really a live wire.

I've lived a life of action
And done all sorts of things.
You see only PD and
The trouble that it brings.

So I just want to tell you,
Don't be put off by my mask,
Seek out the man behind it
Is all that I would ask.

The Parkinson's mask is just one of the many symptoms, both visible and invisible.

Our PD

Your PD gives you the shakes.
Mine gives me a tremor.
Yours has zapped your sense of smell,
Has mine? I can't remember.

His delights in restless legs
To keep him wide awake.
Hers is always freezing
So she's stuck, for goodness sake.

My PD has dulled my voice
Until I'm just a croak.
Theirs likes to wait 'til lunchtime
When it loves to make them choke.

Our PD has closed some doors
Left us in disarray.
Our PD has brought us close –
You can't take that away.

More symptoms, most of which could be seen at the competitions. One of the first games I played at the German Open was against a woman with a very strong tremor which she had to try and bring under control before she could serve the ball. She also had to try and calculate the best time to take her medication so that she was at her best when the time came to play. I wasn't sure what the etiquette was, was it ok to let rip? Of course it was. She got in first, having no such qualms, and beat me hollow.

Factotum

For a team to be successful,
And to help it be its best,
Certain things are needed
If it's to pass the test.

There's the skill of individuals
Honed to a fine degree,
Dedication and hard work too,
I'm sure you will agree.

As well as all the flash bits,
Components need good glue.
Team England have a Gerry
Who knows just what to do.

If you want something finding
Or simply want a knock,
He'll happily oblige
He even functions as our doc.

He's our bearded father figure
Who keeps us all in check
But now he needs to go home
Cos he's a total wreck.

For every person with Parkinson's, there's a carer not far away and their help is invaluable. Gerry somehow managed to look out for three of us for the best part of a fortnight.

Top Man

Top man Andrew Cassy
Leads the best team on the planet.
Their hearts are made of oak
And their heads are made of granite.

He brought us from the UK
And bound us to his side
To challenge would-be upstarts
Who came from far and wide.

We have worked our socks off
And done everything we can
To render unto Cassy
The things we owe this man.

He brought us all this way
and encouraged self-belief.
All hail to Andrew Cassy
We swear loyalty to our Chief!!!

It's all about teamwork.

Lizzie! Lizzie! Lizzie!

I went to the World Championships
And gave it everything I had.
I tried my best to concentrate
And I didn't do too bad.
I absorbed the electric atmosphere
And listened to the cheers,
Heard people calling out my name
Banishing my fears.
Although I didn't do enough
To win a silver or a gold,
I breathed on glowing embers
And a tiny flame took hold.
I'll carry that flame with me
To every future game
As I hear people shouting
And calling out my name.

Lizzie! Lizzie! Lizzie!

International

It all seems totally irrational
Liz is going international
Some would say at sixty eight
She's left it just a wee bit late.
Why would somebody her age
Want to take up centre stage?
Surely now she's past her prime
And may not have a lot of time
She should rest and take it slow
She has got Parkinson's you know.

I'm not about to give up yet
On doing more my heart is set
I don't know what it is I seek
I think I've yet to reach my peak
Although I'm not in tip top form
I'm here and ready to perform
I take it that you feel the same
And that you're here to play the game
So grab your bat if you are able
We'll thrash each other off the table!

German Open, Bad Homburg, May, 2022

Frankfurt Hahn Airport............................ 79
On Safari.. 80
Ping Pong Parkinson Bad Homburg............ 81
German Catering..................................... 83

Frankfurt Hahn Airport

Good bye, auf wiedersehen
We'll not pass this way again
For which I heave a sigh of great relief
The airport Frankfurt Hahn
Of which I'm not a fan
Has been a frantic source of noisy grief.

There's nothing worse than folk
Who jostle, shout and poke
While waiting to stampede towards their plane.
And if I could have my way
I'd send them the wrong way
Or pack them off to Blighty on a train.

The airports are the downside as far as I'm concerned.

On Safari

The noises were rather alarming,
Not what we expected to hear
While sitting with friends in the sunshine
Quietly sipping a beer.

The sounds rattled round the pond's edges,
Harsh squawks were heard up in the trees
It sounds as though we're on safari
It's enough to make your blood freeze.

There's surely a predator out there
Some kind of killing machine
Lusting for blood from its victim
Determined to suck it's bones clean.

With all the stealth we can muster
We stare at the sight, all agog
As there, in the cool of the water
Sings a green, baby faced, two inch frog.

I was challenged to write a poem about the tiny creature that lived in the hotel pond and which made such an awful racket.

Ping Pong Parkinson, Bad Homburg

Ping pong Parkinson
Here we are again
Ping pong Parkinson
Crack open the champagne!

Ping pong Parkinson!
Let's play best of three
Ping pong Parkinson!
Here's the referee

Ping pong Parkinson!
The match is under way
Ping pong Parkinson!
Come and watch them play

Ping pong Parkinson!
Time to serve the ball
Ping pong Parkinson!
The score is two games all

Ping pong Parkinson!
Things are getting hot
Ping pong Parkinson!
What a superb shot

Ping pong Parkinson!
The ball goes in the net
Ping pong Parkinson!
Working up a sweat

Ping pong Parkinson!
Getting in a spin
Ping pong Parkinson!
Who is going to win?

Ping pong Parkinson!
This is gripping stuff
Ping pong Parkinson!
Who has done enough?

Ping pong Parkinson!
Now it's almost done
Ping pong Parkinson!
It's me! It's me! I've won!!

Nenad has declared that I'm now the official PPP poet. This means writing and performing new poems as the competitions progress. I'm amazed at how many players understand English, and especially when delivered in the form of a poem.

German Catering

There's a preoccupation with schnitzel,
The sausage is popular too,
Or you may like to try their potato
If you're looking for something to chew.

Beware, if you're vegetarian
With particular dietary needs,
The nearest you'll get to a carrot
Is a team of bat wielding Swedes.

Sometimes it's difficult to find the food you need.

Portuguese Open, Estoril, June, 2022

Losing It… ………………………. 85
Heavens Above………………….. 86
Gorgeous Jorge………………….. 87
Ping Pong Parkinson Is Coming… 88
Postcard from Portugal………………. 89

Losing It

As the final shot is made, I fix a smile upon my face,
Shake hands with my adversary and leave the court with grace.

But deep inside I'm raging, I want to scream and shout,
Stamp my feet in anger, let my temper out.
Why do I always have to lose? I hardly ever win
and now I've really had enough, my patience has worn thin.
I'd like to tear the net to shreds and squash that stupid ball,
Hurl my worse than useless bat up against the wall!
No one likes bad losers, I know that all too well.
You'd never guess from my demeanour, I wish you all would go to hell.
Be wary when you play me cos one day I may flip
For I am getting closer to the time when I'll let rip.
I know I shouldn't feel like this and take it all to heart,
Believe me when I tell you there's little joy in taking part.

I hear myself pontificate to cover up my shame -
"It doesn't matter if you lose, it's how you play the game.
As long as you enjoy it, it's just a harmless bit of fun
A nice way to keep fit and well when all is said and done."

But watch out and be careful, be sure to watch my bat
Cos one day I'm going to get you - you can be very sure of that!

I actually wrote this at the first Parkinson's UK competition held in St Neots. I've included it here because it's a favourite of our Portuguese friend Damasio.
Games are played with all the competitive fervour you would expect from an international, and also with friendship, compassion and empathy.

Heavens Above

The assault on my ears is relentless
On board Ryanair 's cattle truck.
No chance of a nap or a daydream
Cos they're out to make a quick buck.

You can purchase a nice cup of coffee,
Or perfume if that's more your thing.
You can even donate to a charity -
What great satisfaction that brings.

What I'd really like is some quiet
While I stare at the clouds floating by
And the chance to finally jettison
That kid who's done nothing but cry.

I find air travel noisy, uncomfortable and undignified.

Gorgeous Jorge

Jorge looks bored stiff
As he gives a little sniff
And waves his arms around to show his cuffs.
He knows he must look cool
Because he's no one's fool
And this lot onboard are just a load of scruffs.

He longs for olden days
And more exclusive ways
When passengers were beautiful or rich.
Clark Gable in a suit.
Marlene with cheroot
Or Bette who could sometimes be a bitch.

These days it's screaming hordes
Who come galloping on board
Yelling at their kids to "SETTLE DOWN!".
While they order too much drink
So that they don't have to think
And someone always likes to play the clown.

One day he'll think, that's it
I've had enough, I quit
And at thirty thousand feet he'll prise a door
And all the passengers will shout
As the G-force sucks them out
And they'll never fly with Ryanair no more.

Ping Pong Parkinson is Coming

Ping Pong Parkinson
Ping Pong Parkinson
Ping Pong Parkinson
Ping Pong Parkinson

Ping Pong Parkinson
The word is on the street
Ping Pong Parkinson
Get up and move your feet
Ping Pong Parkinson
The word is spreading round
Ping Pong Parkinson
There's something new in town
Ping Pong Parkinson
Shake along with me
Ping Pong Parkinson
The power will set you free
Ping Pong Parkinson
Let the fighting cease
Ping Pong Parkinson
What we want is peace
Ping Pong Parkinson
Reach out and have some fun
Ping Pong Parkinson
Together we are one.

Ping Pong Parkinson
Ping pong Parkinson
Ping Pong Parkinson
Ping Pong Parkinson

Made for chanting

Postcard from Portugal

Dear Dad,

I'm sending a postcard from Portugal
To say, I wish you were here.
We're having such fun with our Parkinson's
That all of our cares disappear.

We're here in wall-to-wall sunshine,
Ping Pong is what we're about,
It gives us a temporary amnesia,
A welcome relief, there's no doubt.

Damasio's the man of the moment,
He's arranged for us all to meet
So we are the United Nations –
We don't fight, but we like to compete.

I'll show you my holiday photos,
Then you'll see that on everyone's face
Is a smile that surely speaks volumes
As we share hugs and warmly embrace,

Love from Liz xx

World Championships, Pula, Croatia, October, 2022

Level Playing Field………...……………. 91
Security…………………………………... 92
The Ping Pong Man……………………… 93
We Meet Again……………………………94

Level Playing Field

People, get ready to battle!
We've reached that time of year
When from the corners of the earth
Great warriors appear.

In different shapes and sizes,
We represent our lands.
No matter that we tremble
Our bats clasped in our hands.

This is our level playing field,
We're here to play the game.
Yes! We all have Parkinson's,
No reason to feel shame.

You won't see any losers
There's so much that we have won
With our love of life and brave hearts
The tournament's begun.

So good luck to all the players,
We're here to tell our story
And as we face up to the challenges,
May we get to taste true glory.

Security

What is this awful nightmare
Played out for all to see,
Where I am just a number
Which is part of my ID?

My bag is taken from me
As is my watch and jacket
And I wonder if it's worth it
And can I really hack it.

No friendly greetings here,
But a sudden sharp demand
That my shoes must be removed
And I bow to the command.

I'm made to stand for scanning
By a security machine
Checking me for weapons,
But, surprise, surprise, I'm clean.

Welcome to Departures.
It drives us Parkies mad,
We're overwhelmed by chaos
And then we feel real bad.

I'm tempted to go home
But that would be so wrong.
Because I'd miss out on the chance
To play some great ping pong.

Like I say, air travel is undignified. I had taken such great care to pack everything neatly to reduce the stress of searching for things, but I emerged on the other side in total disarray. The worst things to deal with for a person with Parkinson's are buttons, shoelaces, belts and wristwatches.

The Ping Pong Man

There's a silver headed man who appears from time to time
Guitar and ping pong paddle in his hands.
He crosses over time-lines as he travels round the globe
Bringing songs and joy to far off lands.

If you see him, make him welcome for he may just change your life
As he brings his hopeful message to inspire.
There's no need to feel adrift or down without a friend,
He has the very thing that you require.

He knows that there's a key that will manage your PD
And give you back some measure of control.
The friendships that you make will lift your spirits high
And bring you a sweet balm to soothe your soul.

Table tennis is the game that will exercise your mind,
Distract you as you move and play to win.
Your balance will improve as will reaction times
And so your rehabilitation can begin.

So let us thank this man and the vision that he brings
And marvel at what lies beneath his hat.
As he casts the Ping Pong message to all both far and wide
For no one can do any more than that.

Nenad Bach is the man. He is loved, respected and admired by all his PingPongParrkinsons friends.

We Meet Again

Handshakes and hugs,
Cries of delight,
Fist bumps and kisses
As friends reunite.

Thorsten is here
And Nenad is too
To give a warm welcome
To me and to you.

Now everyone's here
Let's see who will win
Without more ado,
Let the ping pong begin!

It's great to see everyone greeting each other at the start of a tournament; we're all so excited! Friendships are made very quickly under these conditions.

Part 3

Parkinson's

	Page
Appeal...	96
Parkinson's..	97
Parkinson's Disease...........................	98
More Parkinson's Disease....................	99
The End...	100
Drifting..	102
My Mind..	103
Self Portrait.......................................	104
You Can Stick It................................	105
Cognitive Impairment..........................	106
Dreamcatcher.....................................	107
Time Waits..	107
If It Wasn't For the Parkinson's...............	109

Appeal

As a person with PD
I'll tell you what it means to me
To be a part of something new
That gives me worthwhile things to do.

Table tennis is the sport
Through which I get such great support.
It keeps me fit. I love the game,
It really sets my soul aflame.

Just when doors were swinging shut,
I saw my future in a rut.
Then I joined the PD team.
Surely this must be a dream?

At every level of the game
Consensus is we feel the same.
What matters is the taking part
That buoys us up and gives us heart.

Through links we've forged with other lands
Our outlook grows, our world expands.
So see things from our point of view,
You'd feel the same now, wouldn't you?

Another fundraising poster

Parkinson's

Diagnosed eight years ago,
Now more symptoms start to show.
No two people are the same
It's like a random guessing game.
I wait with curiosity
To see what it will do to me.
Depending on which cells are lost
Determines what will be the cost.

There is no remedy or cure,
One thing's certain, that's for sure.
Each day it gets a little worse
That's the nature of this curse.
I try to take it on the chin
Stop bad thoughts from creeping in.
I mustn't look too far ahead
But focus on today instead.

This wasn't in my master plan
But I will fight, do what I can
This life's the only one I've got
Now's not the time to lose the plot.
Screams of laughter, not dismay
Are the order of the day.
So there's no need to pity me
Just make me laugh and set me free.

Parkinson's Disease

A neurological condition that likes to use long words,
It's known to be degenerative and can't be cured with herbs.
It's been around for years now and is steadily gaining ground
The numbers are increasing and a cure has not been found.

If you're not familiar with the symptoms of PD,
Let me guide you through a few as they apply to me.
A harmless little tremor was the first thing to appear.
I thought perhaps I'd trapped a nerve so nothing there to fear.

But the doctor wasn't happy and sent me for a scan
And so the long slow path to diagnosis then began.
I had to see a specialist who walked me up and down
And watched me wave my fingers while she looked on with a frown.

All in all it took a year before I knew for sure
That what I had was Parkinson's for which there is no cure.
The shock sat deep within me, I read everything I could
Googling various websites which didn't do me good.

But one thing I was sure of that I'd come to realise
Was that I must keep on moving and take lots of exercise.
You'll find one's smaller movements are the first to disappear
Making buttons pretty tricky and your handwriting unclear.

So do yourself a favour if PD should visit you
Find a good support group who will help to see you through.
Exercise is vital, you should do some every day
And most of all get laughing and keep the blues at bay.

I've been told that if you have to suffer from a neurological disease, Parkinson's is the best one to have. Consolation indeed.

More Parkinson's Disease

Yes, PD affects movement, though that's not the only thing.
There are many other symptoms that this condition brings.
For me, it's how I see things, where they are in space
Multi-tasking's out and I've had to slow my pace.

Doors really are an issue, though they never used to be.
I could open them and close them, they always worked for me.
But now I fight and fumble while they block all my attempts
I can feel their scornful gaze as they treat me with contempt.

It's a similar situation when it comes to using zips,
It takes many clumsy movements 'til I can get a grip
And in the deep midwinter when I am feeling cold,
It takes hours to tuck my vest in cos I struggle to keep hold.

As this brain condition has relentlessly progressed,
I've come to notice some things that now put me to the test.
To empty the dishwasher just seems to take me ages
As I dither over what to do and tackle it in stages.

It's the same thing dishing meals up. Plans often go to pot
Juggling with the saucepans while trying to keep things hot.
I stagger round the kitchen, a curse escapes my lips
As I hear a tell-tale sound that means I've dropped the chips.

To use a layman's terms, the problem seems to lie
With my automatic pilot who now likes to run and hide.
This means I have to really focus on the task or tasks in hand
And take it nice and slow with all the patience I command.

And yet there's a conundrum, one thing that still holds true -
I can still play top speed table tennis and hit the ball on cue.
So every day I grab my bat and then approach the table
And play at ninety miles an hour for which I really am most grateful.

The other cheery thing I've been told is that you don't die of Parkinson's, you die with it.
Great. That means I'm going to get something else.

The End

When I received my diagnosis,
I could barely comprehend.
My life was good as finished,
I thought it was the end.

Wiped clean of adventure
Or trying something new
I must sit and wait for death
That's all that I could do.

Well, what a lot of twaddle
That turned out to be!
There was plenty out there waiting
For someone such as me.

I discovered Nordic walking
For people with PD,
Made plenty of new friends
Very similar to me.

Table tennis was still there,
I continue playing league.
My shots are still improving,
Some are very good indeed.

My rhymes have now been published
Together in a book
Now on sale with Amazon
Don't believe me? Take a look.

Yes, PD made a difference
Set me on another path
Though it's not what I'd have chosen
Perhaps I'm having the last laugh.

What could be any better
Than being here right now
Spouting rhymes to you lot
And now I'll take my bow!

I wrote this when I gave a couple of open air poetry recitals between lockdowns to raise money for Parkinson's

Drifting

I can float for hours and hours and never achieve a thing.
My mind is loose and cast adrift, it takes flight on a wing.

Minutes turn to hours as the day soon melts away
I can't remember what I've done and how I've spent the day.

All my smart to do lists that I once used as a spur
Now simply keep a tally of all the things that I defer.

Procrastination rules me now, my focus has been lost.
If I could be bothered, I'd work out what it costs.

It's not that it's unpleasant, it doesn't leave a taste,
It's just that I'm very conscious that my life is going to waste.

So should I seek an answer, and try to make things change
Or accept that's how it is now and just beyond my range.

My Mind

My mind it is fraying, it feels full of fluff
I try to look clever, but it's all a big bluff.
I once was efficient and did things so fast,
But now I'm a slow coach and usually last.
I drift in a dream world that makes people cross
I remember so little, my former life's lost.
My childhood has vanished, my youth is a blur
My sister remembers, I wish I was her.
I peer at the future, it doesn't look good
How will I cope with a head made of wood?
Will I be useless and shuffle about?
Cry with frustration and constantly shout?
Or will I smile sweetly and be a good girl
Do what I'm told while I gently unfurl?
Don't know how to end this, to guess what comes next
All I can do is hope for the best.

Self Portrait

A glance into the mirror shows
A few fine lines around my nose.
My face is framed with shaggy hair
I'm falling into disrepair.

The world does battle with my skin,
My once plump lips are pale and thin,
Eyelids droop, hide tired eyes
Failing sight is no surprise.

Yet inside I'm still the same,
Still keen to play life's fickle game
As though forever twentyone
On the lookout still for fun.

Where's the girl who used to play
Run riot with her friends all day
And liked to stay out half the night
Come creeping home in the dawn light,

Of these things there is no trace
On my Parkinson's steely face
But don't be put off by my gaze
It's just that I've seen better days.

You Can Stick It!

Tomorrow? You can stick it -
I'd rather have the past,
When I was young and carefree
And the pace of life was fast.

I giggled with my girlfriends
And chased after the boys,
Everything was funny
And we made a lot of noise.

We had no thought of illness
Or ever growing old.
We wore skimpy little tops
And never felt the cold.

We hurtled round the neighbourhood
And didn't give a damn,
Tried smoking by the bike sheds
Always poised to scram.

Half a century later
All signs of youth have gone.
My joints are stiff and painful
And my skin is pale and wan.

Parkinson's is here now,
I've got arthritis too.
If I get dementia
I don't know what I'll do.

In the lottery of health
I've drawn a losing ticket
The future's looking grim
Tomorrow? You can stick it!

Most of the time I manage to stay positive, but now and again I like to hit out.

Cognitive Impairment

Cognitive impairment.
What exactly does it mean?
Although it isn't painful,
I'm really not that keen.

They say it's not dementia,
It's not like that at all,
Though some automatic skills
Might now begin to stall.

Your former powers of recall
Might show a slow decline
And tap dancing while juggling
Aren't the best skills to combine.

There are issues too with maths,
The figures won't add up
As the numbers roll about
Like a frisky playful pup.

You live life in slow motion
And time just disappears.
Being left behind is
Now your biggest fear.

Your many friends and family
Are quick to smile and nod
As they rush to hide the fact
That they think you're getting odd.

Might as well embrace it,
Make out it doesn't matter.
I'm an understudy to
The proverbial Mad Hatter.

There is a school of thought that says a lot of people with Parkinson's go on to develop creative abilities such as poetry, prose, painting, drawing and photography. It's certainly a form of consolation for me.

Dreamcatcher

The rush of thoughts I have each day
Spills out in such a random way.
I often feel I'm in a trance
Watching ideas swirl and dance.

My thoughts and feelings mesmerise,
They bob and weave before my eyes.
I know if I don't write them down
They'll disappear, and go to ground.

I find I have to be prepared
Now my memory's so impaired.
That's why I scribble lots in books
Making notes that act like hooks.

I list the things that I must do
To get me through each day anew.
And then of course there are my rhymes -
Oddball ideas and half baked lines.

These must be caught with pen and ink
Or they'll be gone, quick as a wink.
But how am I to read my scrawl
Now that my writing's very small?

Strange shapes that look like hieroglyphs
Gather in great heaps and drifts
They stretch themselves across the page
Deciphering them takes an age.

This is how I write my verse
My methods can be quite perverse
Gradually I'm getting worse
Time for my medication, NURSE!

Time Waits …

"Wait half a sec". " Hang on a mo".
"I'll be with you in a tick".
These phrases now mean nothing
As I'm anything but quick.

The thief we know as Parkinson's
Has stolen time away.
Things that once took minutes,
Now seem to take all day.

Two hours to make a cottage pie,
All morning just to shop,
As for changing duvets -
Make the torture stop.

I'm living in a dream world,
I'm being left behind.
I have the strangest feeling
That I'm starting to unwind.

I'll end up like a statue
With no outer sign of life.
People will point at me and say
That I'm Lot's second wife.

If It Wasn't For The Parkinson's

If it wasn't for the Parkinson's, I wouldn't have the shakes
And all the other symptoms and the trouble that it makes.

If it wasn't for the Parkinson's, I'd get to sleep at night
Instead of counting sheep, getting more and more uptight.

If it wasn't for the Parkinson's, I wouldn't write daft rhyme,
I'd do things that were sensible and worthy of my time.

If it wasn't for the Parkinson's, there'd be no books of verse,
Could it be this illness is a blessing, not a curse?

If it wasn't for the Parkinson's I wouldn't be here now
Performing on the world stage, about to take a bow.

If it wasn't for the Parkinson's, you wouldn't be my friend,
Someone I can laugh with and on whom I can depend.

If it wasn't for the Parkinson's …

Printed in Great Britain
by Amazon